my healthy habits

Look Out for Germs!

Published in the United States of America by Cherry Lake Publishing
Ann Arbor, Michigan
www.cherrylakepublishing.com

Reading Adviser: Marla Conn MS, Ed., Literacy specialist, Read-Ability, Inc.
Book Design: Jennifer Wahl
Illustrator: Jeff Bane

Library of Congress Cataloging-in-Publication Data

Names: Marsico, Katie, 1980- author. | Bane, Jeff, 1957- illustrator.
Title: Look out for germs! / by Katie Marsico ; [illustrator] Jeff Bane.
Description: Ann Arbor, Michigan: Cherry Lake Publishing, [2019] | Series: My healthy habits | Audience: K to grade 3. | Includes bibliographical references and index. Identifiers: LCCN 2018034525| ISBN 9781534142817 (hardcover) | ISBN 9781534140578 (pdf) | ISBN 9781534139374 (pbk.) | ISBN 9781534141773 (hosted ebook) Subjects: LCSH: Microbiology--Juvenile literature. | Bacteria--Juvenile literature. Classification: LCC QR57 .M38 2019 | DDC 579--dc23
LC record available at https://lccn.loc.gov/2018034525

Printed in the United States of America
Corporate Graphics

table of contents

About the author: Katie Marsico is the author of more than 200 reference books for children and young adults. She lives with her husband and six children near Chicago, Illinois.

About the illustrator: Jeff Bane and his two business partners own a studio along the American River in Folsom, California, home of the 1849 Gold Rush. When Jeff's not sketching or illustrating for clients, he's either swimming or kayaking in the river to relax.

Photo Credits: ©TY Lim/Shutterstock, 5; ©pixinoo/Shutterstock, 7; ©plantic/Shutterstock, 9; ©Vipada Kanajod/Shutterstock, 11; ©A3pfamily/Shutterstock, 13; ©angellodeco/Shutterstock, 15; ©Oksana Kuzmina/Shutterstock, 17; ©Africa Studio/Shutterstock, 19; ©GUNDAM_Ai/ Shutterstock 21; ©wavebreakmedia/Shutterstock, 23; Cover, 6, 10, 12, Jeff Bane; Various vector images throughout courtesy of Shutterstock.com/Irina Iglina and Macrovector

Have you ever cracked an egg while cooking?

What happens when you're done?

You wash your hands!

We should always wash hands before and after handling **raw** food. This helps stop the spread of **germs**.

Germs make us sick.

Some live on hard **surfaces**.

Others are found in **fluids** or in the air.

How do you avoid getting sick?

Germs spread fast in bathrooms. They also live in kitchens and trash cans.

Some pets spread germs, too.

So do wild animals.

Sick people can spread germs.

Germs travel when we cough and sneeze. They also pass through body fluids.

What do you do when you sneeze?

Looking out for germs isn't enough. We need to **avoid** them.

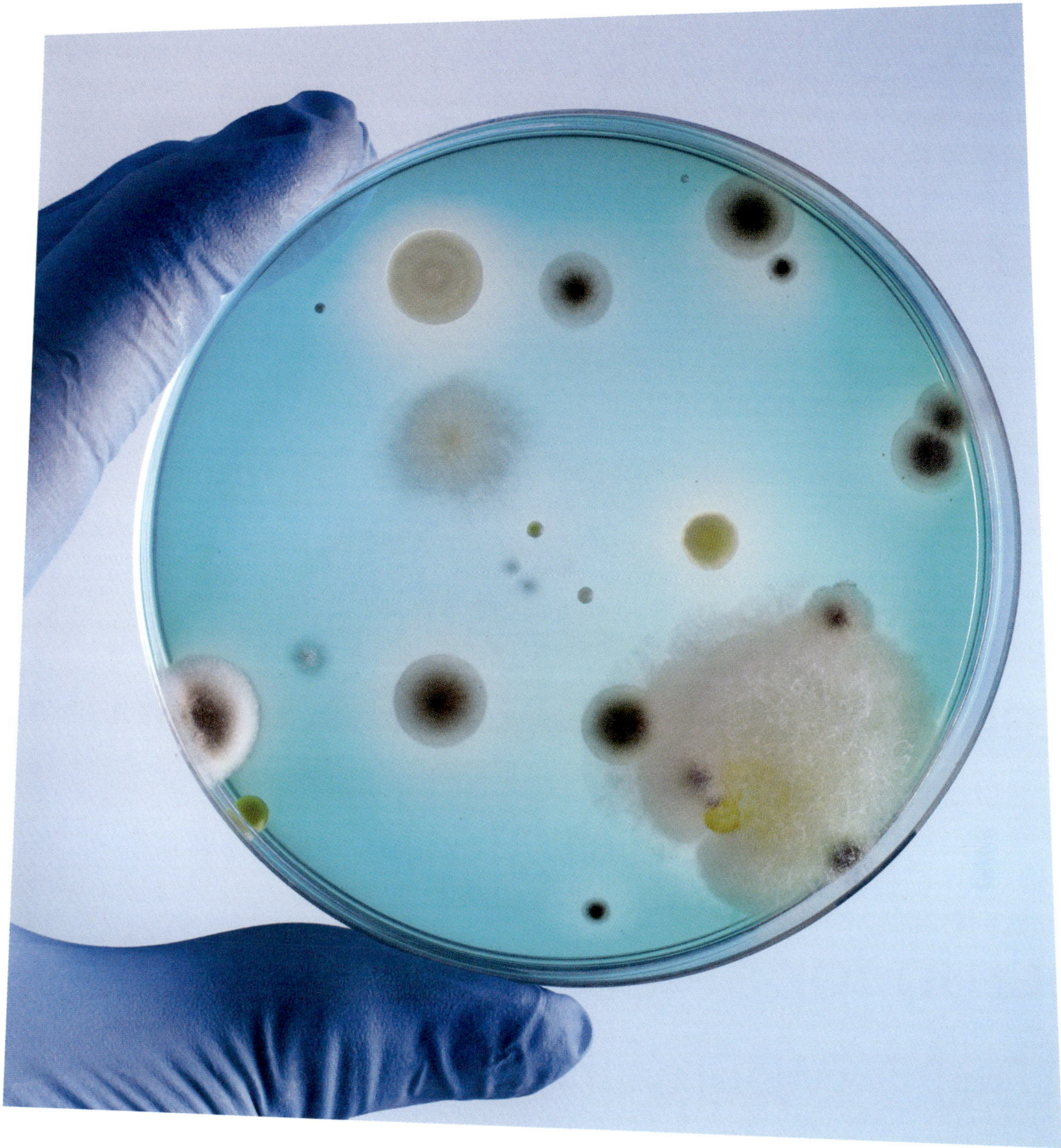

Hand washing is a good start.

Use soap and water.

Scrub for at least 20 seconds. (That’s two rounds of the “Happy Birthday” song.)

Find out how to clean different spaces. Ask how adults **disinfect** them.

Always follow directions when handling food. Do the same when caring for pets.

Is someone at school sneezing a lot?

Don't touch what they touch! Wash your hands instead!

Ask your doctor for more tips for staying well.

Germs are all around us. Watching out for them will give you a healthy future!

What are some of your healthy habits?

glossary & index

glossary

avoid (uh-VOYD) to keep away from

disinfect (dis-in-FEKT) to clean an area or object by destroying the germs living within it

fluids (FLOO-uhdz) liquids with no fixed shape

germs (JURMZ) tiny organisms that often cause disease

raw (RAW) uncooked or undercooked

surfaces (SUHR-fuhs-uz) the outside or outer layers of something

index